GERMANY
THE REUNIFICATION OF A NATION

CATHERINE AND JOHN BRADLEY

A GLOUCESTER PRESS BOOK

Contents

Introduction

On 3 October 1990 East and West Germany were reunited to form a new Germany. This marked the end of 45 years of division between East and West, following the Second World War. The new Germany is Europe's most powerful economy. West Germany is the dominant partner in the reunification process and most of the East German institutions have been swallowed up by West German ones.

The new Germany is a smaller version of the original German empire which was unified in 1871. The architect of that unification was Prince Otto von Bismarck, the Prussian prime minister. From 18 January 1871 all the Prussians, Hanoverians, Hessians, Bavarians and Saxons became Germans within the new German empire (known as the Second Reich or empire).

Germany was officially divided after the end of the Second World War in 1949 into the German Federal Republic in the West and the smaller German Democratic Republic in the East. West Germany developed as a democracy with several parties standing for government in elections. It had a market economy in which businesses were allowed to operate without too much government interference. West Germany was part of the European Community and had close links with its neighbours in Western Europe. It was also a member of the North Atlantic Treaty Organisation which allied it with the United States. East Germany had a communist system of government with overall control in the hands of the Socialist Unity Party. The party ran the state as well as businesses and East Germany's land and resources. It was allied to the Soviet Union and traded with the other communist countries of Eastern Europe.

The new, united Germany is one of today's hotspots because it lies at the centre of Europe. During the 20th century it has fought in two world wars and many people are afraid that a strong Germany will dominate Europe. For the next few years other European countries will be watching events in Germany to make sure their worst fears are not confirmed. The cost of reuniting Germany will be high because East German industry will have to be completely rebuilt. Many West Germans resent having to pay for this. East Germans are unhappy about their low wages and poor standard of living. Although East and West Germans share the same language, there are enormous differences between them. The tension between East and West Germans will take years to disappear.

▽ On the night of 3 October 1990 crowds of people assembled on the steps of the *Reichstag* building in the heart of Berlin to celebrate German reunification. The *Reichstag* was where the German parliament met before 1933. It was greatly damaged during the Second World War but it still stood as an empty monument. It was a symbol of a democratic united Germany which has finally been achieved in 1990.

3

Blood and unity

In 1871 Germany became united under the Prussian kings in the Second Reich. In the early part of the 20th century it drifted into war.

△ In 1648 the Thirty Years War came to an end with the signing of the Peace of Münster with France and Osnabrück with Sweden. The war had been extremely bloody and it took the Germans many years to recover.

The first advocate of German unification was the Frankish King Charlemagne, who reigned in 800 AD. He extended his empire to include much of France and western Germany, as well as northern Italy. Within a generation after Charlemagne's death, his sons and grandsons divided his Holy Roman Empire (the original First Reich) into numerous kingdoms and princedoms. It remained disunited for over a thousand years.

The Holy Roman Empire of the German Nation was the most important power in Central Europe in the Middle Ages. It included many kingdoms, dukedoms and principalities. The leading rulers of these units elected one of their number to be the Holy Roman Emperor. During the 16th century, religious and social differences brought conflict to the Holy Roman Empire. Martin Luther, a German monk, challenged the Catholic Church's teachings. He was thrown out of the Catholic Church and developed his own religious ideas, called Protestantism. Many other religious leaders followed him in criticising Catholicism, and Europe divided between Catholics and Protestants.

Religious wars broke out throughout Europe. Within the Holy Roman Empire there was a war for control of Central Europe which involved Sweden and France. Many Germans aspired to unity in one real German empire (Reich) rather than in the existing, but very weak, Holy Roman one. However, these hopes for German unification seemed unrealisable and, in 1648, at the end of the Thirty Years War, Germany was made up of some 230 kingdoms, principalities and free towns. Its economy was in ruins and one-third of its population had been killed in the war.

▽ Frederick the Great leads his victorious troops into battle against Austria. He was the king of Prussia from 1740-86. He fought several wars against Austria and gained much Polish territory for Prussia.

Unifying Germany

One state that recovered and grew in power was Prussia. The Prussian kings built up their army, which was used in many wars in the 18th and 19th centuries, and made Berlin the Prussian capital. In the early 19th century Prussia rallied the Germans to help defeat the French emperor, Napoleon I. In 1815 the great European powers that had defeated Napoleon – Prussia, Austria, Russia and Britain – met at the Congress of Vienna, where they established a German confederation of largely independent states.

The year 1848 was a year of revolutions when people all over Europe rose up because they wanted to get rid of their monarchs. In Germany the people's cry was for unification. The appeal of nationalism – the desire of a group of peoples sharing a common language or culture to govern themselves – was on the increase. The southern Germans, however, wanted a Reich which included Austria, while the northern Germans were not keen on a Germany that included all the peoples of the Austrian empire. A national assembly met in Frankfurt in May 1848 and tried to resolve these problems. In March 1849 the assembly decided that what was needed was an emperor and offered the crown to Frederick William IV of Prussia. He turned it down because he did not want to accept a crown offered by "revolutionaries".

Shortly after this episode, Frederick William went mad and his brother succeeded to the throne. In 1862 he called on Otto von Bismarck, an East Prussian landowner, to become the new prime minister of Prussia. Bismarck was a statesman who vowed to use "iron and blood" to bring all the German peoples together under the Prussian monarchy. Bismarck was known as the Iron Chancellor.

Bismarck prepared the way for reunification with three short wars. In 1863 Prussia defeated Denmark in its attempt to annex Schleswig-Holstein, which now forms Germany's northernmost state. In 1866 the Prussian army swiftly defeated the Austrian armies and neutralised Austria's influence in Germany. Bismarck made the most of this and drew Hanover, Saxony and the north German states into the North German Federation. France was alarmed by the rise of a powerful, united Germany and the swift defeat of the French at the battle of Sedan confirmed Prussia's dominance of Germany. The spoils of war included the Catholic Rhineland (as well as Alsace and Lorraine) so that by 1871 Prussia's territory amounted to five-eighths of the new Reich.

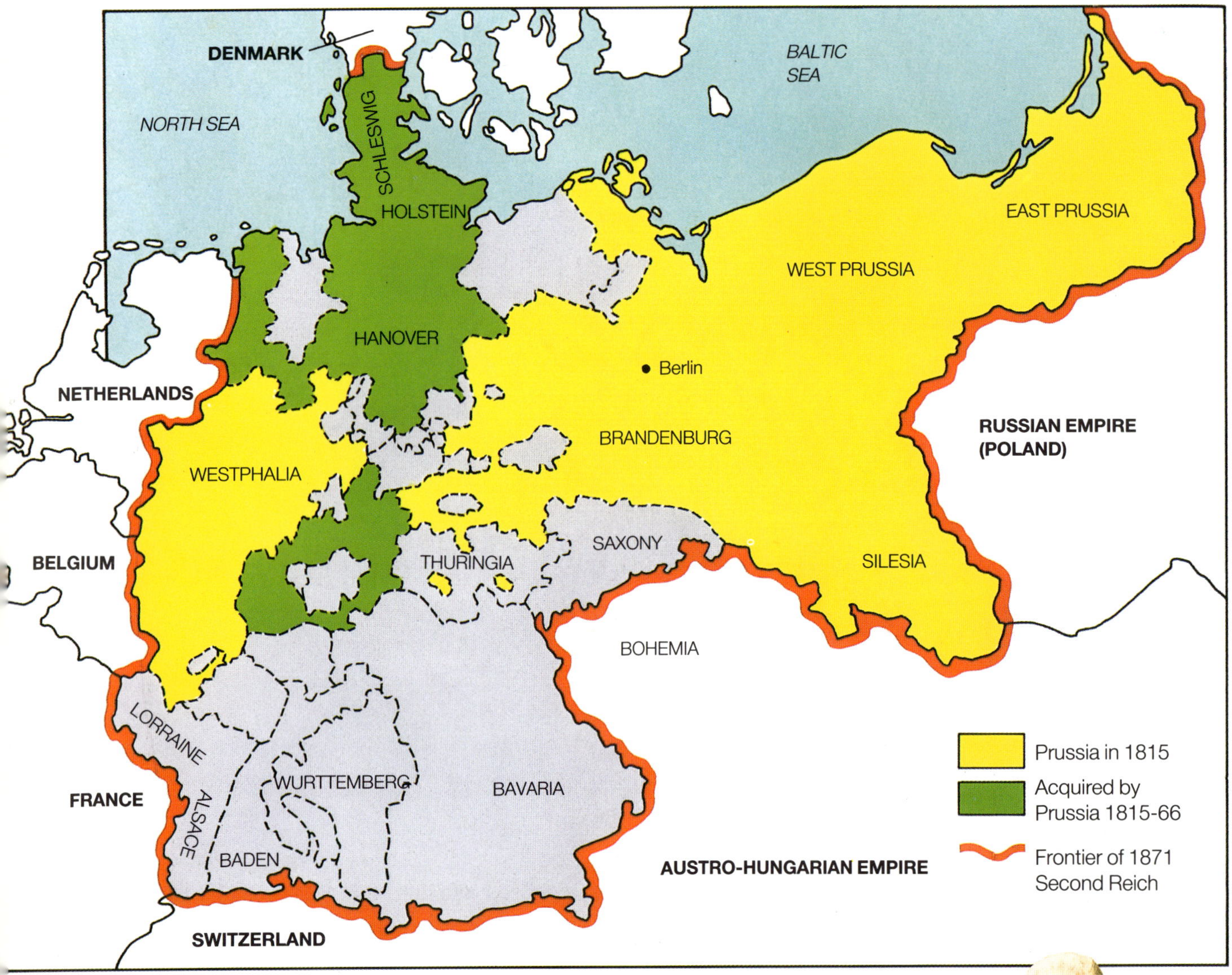

Map

DENMARK

NORTH SEA

BALTIC SEA

SCHLESWIG

HOLSTEIN

HANOVER

EAST PRUSSIA

WEST PRUSSIA

• Berlin

BRANDENBURG

RUSSIAN EMPIRE (POLAND)

NETHERLANDS

WESTPHALIA

BELGIUM

THURINGIA

SAXONY

SILESIA

BOHEMIA

LORRAINE

ALSACE

WURTTEMBERG

BAVARIA

FRANCE

BADEN

AUSTRO-HUNGARIAN EMPIRE

SWITZERLAND

Prussia in 1815

Acquired by Prussia 1815-66

Frontier of 1871 Second Reich

The Second Reich

On 18 January 1871 Germany became a unified country. The announcement was made in the Hall of Mirrors at the Palace of Versailles in France. Bismarck installed William I as Kaiser, (the German word for Caesar) or emperor, of Germany. The newly united German Reich contained many contradictions. German unity had not come about because the people wanted it; the decision was made by princes. The *Bundesrat*, an imperial council headed by the Kaiser, was made up of the princes and princelings of the reunited states. The German liberals, who were the driving force for reunification, were given a parliament (*Reichstag*) which was to be elected by the people, since all men had a vote. However, it had very little power: it could only delay laws it did not approve, and every seventh year it could refuse to pass the army's budget.

The map shows the boundaries of the Second Reich in 1871. Prussia had long been the dominant German nation. It had acquired Silesia, Brandenburg and Westphalia before 1815. Between 1815-66 it gained Hanover and in 1871 it took Alsace and Lorraine from France. Many Germans were disappointed that the united Germany did not include the Austro-Hungarian empire.

△ William II was the last German Kaiser. His reign lasted from 1888-1918. He was related to most of the European royal families by marriage but that did not prevent Germany from embarking on the First World War with France, Britain and Russia in 1914.

◁ Prince Otto von Bismarck came from a wealthy landowning family and was very conservative. He believed in strengthening Prussia's armies. After less than ten years as chancellor of Prussia he succeeded in negotiating the unification of Germany.

The real power rested with the imperial chancellor. He was supreme in both domestic and foreign affairs. Bismarck was the first chancellor and he coped successfully with the increasing power of opposition socialists, sometimes giving them concessions, sometimes repressing them. He was particularly successful in foreign affairs and in 1879 he managed to tie Austria-Hungary to the Reich in exchange for Germany's support for Austria-Hungary's territorial claims in the Balkans (south-eastern Europe). Yet, despite these successes Bismarck's power depended directly on the emperor who appointed and dismissed chancellors without consulting the *Reichstag*.

The new Kaiser

In 1888 William II became the new German Kaiser. He was a young man, impulsive and intelligent, who from the start had difficulties with the old chancellor. After two years he forced Bismarck to resign and looked for a suitable replacement. However, none of his prime ministers came up to his expectations and William II became more and more involved in exercising power directly, particularly in foreign affairs.

Bismarck had based his foreign policy on two principles: a close alliance with Austria-Hungary and friendly relations with Russia. This arrangement helped maintain a balance of power between Germany and France, the historical rivals in Europe. At first William II tried to follow Bismarck's policy, even though the world situation had changed. By the 1900s Austria-Hungary was being torn apart by nationalism as all the nationalities demanded self-government. Austria-Hungary was no longer a strong ally, and Russia had become more of a threat because it had made an alliance with France. However, William II persisted in maintaining close ties with Austria-Hungary, despite the fact it was near collapse.

On the eve of the First World War, Germany found itself in the unenviable position of protecting the ramshackle Austro-Hungarian empire. Austria became involved in conflicts with some neighbouring countries in the Balkans. In turn Russia had put itself forward as the Slav protector of the Balkan nations. The likely outcome of this situation was that the two protectors, Germany and Russia, would come into conflict. This situation undermined Bismarck's principle of maintaining good terms with Russia in order to avoid fighting a war on two fronts (against France in the west and Russia in the east).

The steps to the First World War

William II's arrogance annoyed the Russian royal family, particularly the young Tsar Nicholas II, who had become Russia's ruler in 1894. The two rulers were cousins and in 1905 they met to smooth out their differences. However, they soon discovered that they were not entirely in control of the situation.

In June 1914, the Austrian Crown Prince, Franz Ferdinand, was assassinated by a Serbian nationalist at Sarajevo in the Balkans. Serbia was an independent country but Serbian nationalists wanted Serbia to acquire parts of Austria-Hungary. Serbia was sent an ultimatum demanding an apology for the outrage committed by one of its citizens. When Serbia partially apologised, Austria declared war on her all the same. Russia, Serbia's ally and protector, ordered its army to prepare for war and in turn Germany issued an ultimatum: if Russia did not stop preparing for war, then Germany would declare war on Russia. France in turn prepared for war and Germany declared war on France. Britain then was brought into the war as France's ally when Germany invaded neutral Belgium. In this way Germany was dragged into a war on two fronts by Austria. Bismarck's policies lay in ruin; much greater devastation would follow.

War on two fronts

To start with, it seemed that Germany could cope with fighting on two fronts. The Prussian High Command had devised war plans to cover this. The Schlieffen plan envisaged massing the main bulk of the German armies on the Western Front and invading France through neutral Belgium. After a quick campaign in France, Germany would then face the inferior Russian armies in the east.

△ The news of the outbreak of war in 1914 was greeted with great enthusiasm by many Germans. Their love of their country made them keen to fight a war against France, Germany's traditional enemy. However, no one expected the war to drag on for four hard years. By the end of that time most German people were enduring great hardships as food and raw materials began to run out.

Anti-German propaganda

During the First World War, the British and French newspapers conducted a violent anti-German campaign to keep people's spirits up. The Germans were called the Huns or the *Boches* in French. They were made out to be inhuman demons who ate babies. There was even a report of Belgian priests being used as live clappers to ring bells. These stories were made up, but they gave rise to strong anti-German feelings which persist to this day.

△ In March 1918, the German generals launched a final offensive to try to break the stalemate and win the war. The spring offensives went well at first, and by early June, German troops were within 60 km of Paris. By July, however, the Germans had lost 973,000 men and over a million were sick. The Allies had greater reserves of manpower and this was decisive in their victory. The Germans lost the war on the battlefield and not, as German nationalists claimed, because of unrest at home.

However, the Russian armies moved swiftly across to threaten East Prussia so troops had to be sent east. The Russians were soundly defeated by the Germans at the Battle of Tannenberg, but the Austrian and Hungarian armies were defeated by the Russians in Galicia and by the Serbs in Serbia. The German campaign into France met with initial success but some 100 km short of Paris it ground to a halt. As the German and Anglo-French forces dug into defensive positions, the war became unwinnable. Attack after attack was launched, but neither side could gain the decisive advantage because their firepower was evenly matched.

Germany had not been prepared for a lengthy conflict. Since it could not win decisively either in the west or in the east the war dragged on, fought by soldiers dug into trenches. The British navy enforced a naval blockade which was slowly starving Germany of vital raw materials. The collapse of Russia in 1917, when the war-weary Russians rose up and overthrew their Tsar in the Russian Revolution, gave the Germans some hope. However, by this point the United States had come into the war against Germany, and it was this influx of American soldiers which finally won the war in the west.

By the end of the First World War the Russian, Austro-Hungarian and German empires had ceased to exist. Kaiser William II left for Holland in disgrace and the politicians took over in the chaotic conditions following the German surrender. The new German republic lost Alsace-Lorraine to France and vast territories in the east, mainly to the newly reconstituted Poland. The war left Germany in chaos and many Germans had grievances against the peace terms. It was not long before the German people would be demanding the restoration of the lost territories.

Defeat and division

Following its defeat in the First World War, Germany lost territory to the French and Poles. Germany became divided as right and left fought for power. In 1933 the right under Hitler won and tried to create a Greater Germany, but this led to the Second World War.

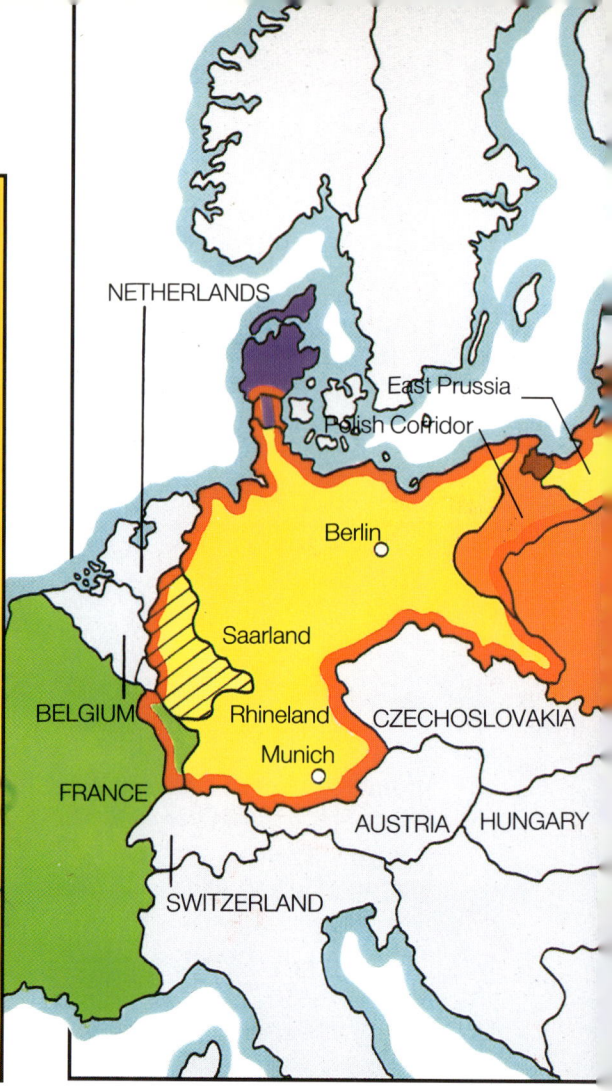

In 1918 the German High Command, led by General Erich Ludendorff and Field Marshal Paul von Hindenburg, told Kaiser William II to ask for an armistice, because they believed their armies could not withstand the next offensive. William responded by trying to reform the German Reich: he appointed a new prime minister, Prince Max von Baden, and made him responsible to the *Reichstag*. However, there were mutinies in Kiel and Berlin as soldiers and sailors attacked their superiors. In these chaotic conditions one of the leaders of the largest party in the German parliament, the Social Democrats, proclaimed a new democratic republic. The Kaiser abdicated and went into exile. The new republic immediately faced a crisis when the extreme left, known as the Spartacists, tried to seize power. The Spartacists were massacred by ex-soldiers, who had joined right-wing private armies, known as the *Freikorps*.

In spite of the chaos a free election was held in January 1919 to elect a constituent assembly which would draft a democratic constitution. The assembly met in Weimar, where conditions were more peaceful and so became known

FINLAND
LITHUANIA
LATVIA
ESTONIA

◁ The map shows the "new" Germany following the 1919 Versailles Treaty. Germany was split into two: East Prussia and the bulk of Germany were separated by Polish land.

▮ German frontier in 1914
▮ Germany
▮ France (with Alsace-Lorraine)
▮ New Polish state
▮ New Lithuanian state
▮ Area under League of Nations
▮ Denmark (with Schleswig-Holstein)
▨ Area under occupation

▽ Sailors take up guard posts in Berlin in December 1918. Many unemployed sailors and soldiers joined private armies in 1918 and this led to fighting.

as the Weimar Republic. The Social Democrats were the largest party in the assembly with 163 seats, but they could not run the country without the support of other parties. The voting system of proportional representation (giving a party the same percentage of seats as the percentage of the votes it received) meant it was difficult for a single party to win a majority. Some 28 parties gained seats in the new parliament but the parties found it difficult to make long-lasting arrangements to govern the country. Coalition governments changed, on average, every seven months.

As well as political instability, the end of the war brought other problems. Inflation meant that prices rose at an alarming rate. The peace terms involved huge reparations (payments to the victorious countries). There was also fighting on the streets as both left-wing and right-wing forces tried to seize power.

The Weimar Republic

Germany seemed on the verge of collapse. The nationalist right-wing accused the Social Democrats of being responsible for Germany's defeat in the First World War by stirring up unrest at home (known as the "stab in the back"). The French occupied the Rhineland and the Ruhr in 1923 when Germany failed to make its reparation payments.

Left-wing and right-wing coup attempts succeeded each other: in 1923 an unknown leader of the National Socialist German Workers' Party (Nazi), Adolf Hitler, failed in organising a coup. He spent the next year in jail and decided to try to gain power legally. Before the First World War, the Austrian Hitler had lived in Vienna, where he had learned to despise Jewish people. He thought the German people (*Volk*) were the master race and should dominate the "inferior" races, such as the Slavs. He also declared that the German Jews, rich and poor alike, were responsible for all the ills that Germany had suffered since 1914. During the 1920s, Hitler built up support for the Nazi movement.

However, Gustav Stresemann, a liberal nationalist, formed a coalition in 1923 and gradually was able to solve the Weimar Republic's most pressing problems. He stopped inflation, which was out of control, with the help of American loans. Stresemann then became foreign minister and renegotiated the reparations payments. He also got Germany admitted into the League of Nations (the international organisation set up in 1919 to secure world peace) and persuaded France and Britain to withdraw their troops from the Rhineland.

Hitler's rise to power

In 1925, the 78-year-old Marshal von Hindenburg was elected president of the republic. He was an important figurehead but he was a very old-fashioned thinker who disliked democracy and wanted to restore the Kaiser. In 1929 the Weimar Republic faced the ultimate crisis; the world economy collapsed with the Wall Street Crash and Stresemann, exhausted by his efforts, died.

In 1929, unemployment in Germany jumped from 1.5 million to 2.5 million and continued to rise. The communists and Nazis saw a chance of winning power by exploiting mass unemployment and began fighting on the streets. Nazi paramilitary troops gradually won the upper hand and in 1930 the Nazi representation in the *Reichstag* jumped from 12 to 107 seats. By 1932, unemployment reached six million and Hitler thought the time had come to achieve power. He stood against Hindenburg in a presidential election and polled 13.3 million votes. Hindenburg won the second round of the election when left-wing voters supported him.

In July 1932 there was another general election since the chancellors appointed by Hindenburg could not get a majority of votes in parliament to support their policies. This time Hitler promised his electors that a few months after a victorious election he would eliminate "the terrorists and oppressors of the German people", who had been in power since 1918. The Nazis gained 230 seats out of 608 and were the largest party in parliament. Hitler had to wait another 18 months before Hindenburg unexpectedly appointed him his chancellor on 30 January 1933. Hindenburg's advisers had assured him that Hitler could easily be kept under control.

▷ During the 1920s, paper money became so worthless that it was used by children to play with. Inflation meant prices rose and rose and paper money lost its value. In January 1921, one dollar was worth 15.5 marks. By December 1922, a dollar was worth 1,810 marks. Goods were often bought by exchanging other goods and those who had nothing to exchange could not buy food, fuel or other essential items.

◁ Gustav Stresemann served as chancellor and foreign minister of the Weimar Republic from 1923-29. He was a realist and understood that he needed to improve Germany's relations with its former enemies so that it could recover from the war and build up its power again. He achieved several successes in negotiating easier terms for the payment of reparations.

▽ Adolf Hitler, Germany's new chancellor, greets President von Hindenburg at an official ceremony in March 1933. Hindenburg took his time before he appointed Hitler. He was advised by privileged men like himself. They looked down on Hitler, who had been a mere corporal in the army and was the son of a customs official. In the end, Hindenburg made Hitler chancellor because his advisers thought they could use Hitler. They were proved wrong.

Hitler's Germany

A month later the *Reichstag* building was mysteriously burned down. Using this as a pretext, Hitler rounded up the left, particularly the communists, and interned them in concentration camps. Next he called an immediate election and gained 288 seats; he demanded special powers from the newly elected *Reichstag*.

Within a year Hitler had eliminated not only his enemies, but also his critics within the Nazi Party, the paramilitary force known as the SA (*Sturm Abteilungen*, or storm troopers). Hitler's own bodyguard, the SS (*Schutz Staffeln*), accomplished this on the Night of the Long Knives in 1934. Hitler became Germany's *Führer* (leader) because he controlled both the state and the army. He had his trusted followers, Hermann Goering and Joseph Goebbels, in key government positions, and Nazi Party members seized power in the administration, schools and universities as well as in the newspapers, magazines and theatres. The churches lost their independence. Jewish people lost their rights and life became more and more difficult as they were attacked by Nazi thugs. Many decided to leave Germany. Trade unionists, homosexuals, gypsies and other "undesirables" were also persecuted and sent to camps. However, the majority of Germans felt Hitler had given them stability.

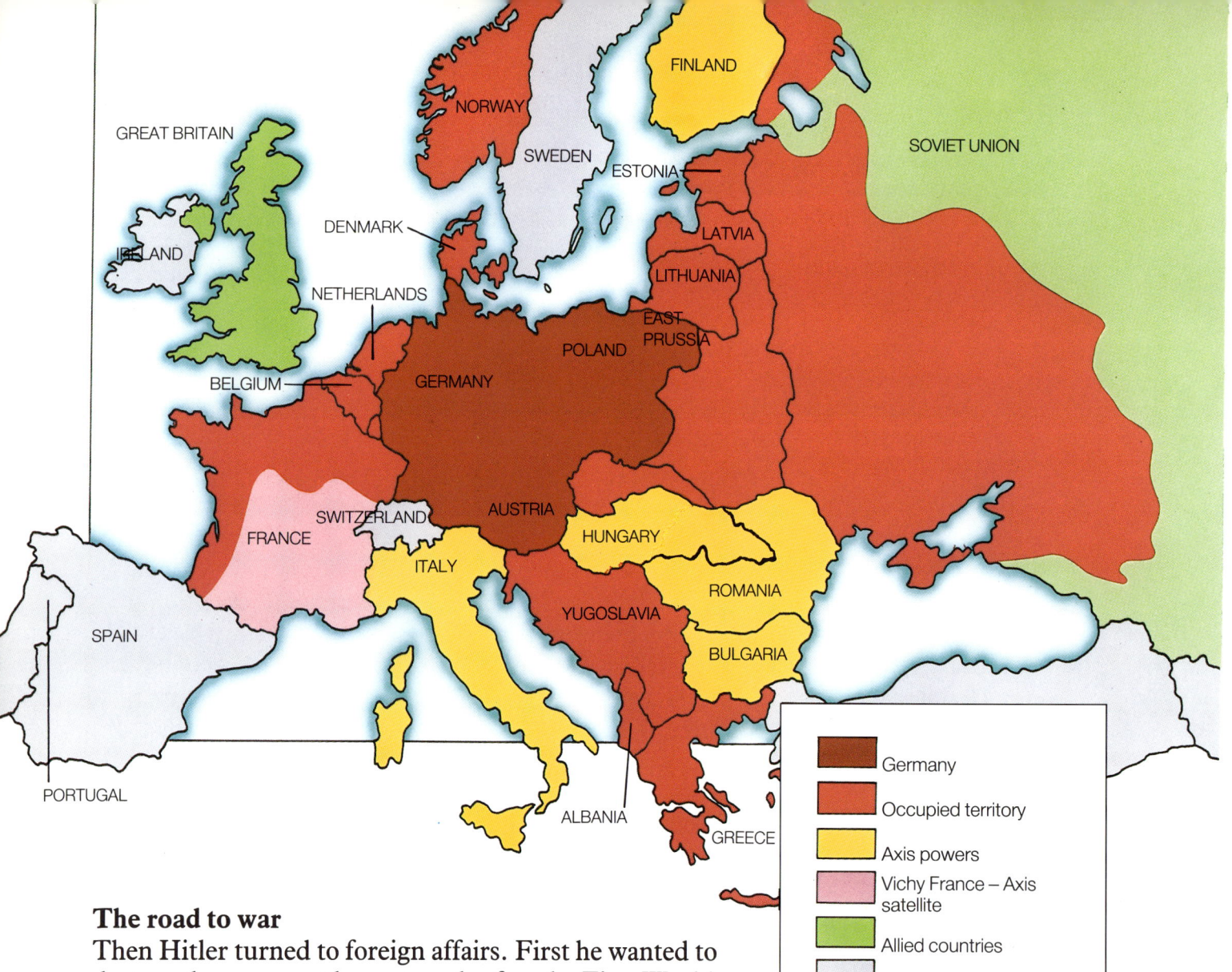

GREAT BRITAIN

NORWAY

FINLAND

SWEDEN

ESTONIA

SOVIET UNION

IRELAND

DENMARK

LATVIA

LITHUANIA

NETHERLANDS

EAST PRUSSIA

POLAND

BELGIUM

GERMANY

SWITZERLAND

FRANCE

AUSTRIA

HUNGARY

ITALY

ROMANIA

SPAIN

YUGOSLAVIA

BULGARIA

PORTUGAL

ALBANIA

GREECE

🟫	Germany
🟥	Occupied territory
🟨	Axis powers
🟪	Vichy France – Axis satellite
🟩	Allied countries
⬜	Neutral countries

The road to war

Then Hitler turned to foreign affairs. First he wanted to destroy the peace settlement made after the First World War, the Versailles Treaty. German troops occupied the Rhineland and recovered the Saar in 1935 and 1936. After that came a series of annexations to reunite the German people and give substance to Hitler's slogan "*Ein Volk, ein Reich, ein Führer*" (One people, one empire, one leader). Austria was annexed outright in 1938, Czechoslovakia's Sudeten lands followed, and the whole of Czechoslovakia became a German protectorate in March 1939.

When he began to claim territories lost to Poland, France and Britain finally warned him that annexation by force would lead to war. Hitler did not believe that the former Allies in the First World War meant what they said. They had done nothing to stop his troops invading other countries except negotiate agreements, which he did not keep to. He concluded a friendship alliance with another European dictator, Joseph Stalin of the Soviet Union, and within a fortnight invaded Poland to incorporate its Germans into his Third Reich, which he claimed would last a thousand years.

The map shows the extent of Hitler's Third Reich by the summer of 1942. Only Britain and the Soviet Union were left in the war against Germany in Europe. Spain, Sweden and Switzerland were all neutral. Outside Europe, Germany had lost all its colonies, but its ally Japan had made sweeping conquests in the Far East. Japan's attack on the US naval base at Pearl Harbor brought the United States into the war. The American contribution was decisive in defeating Germany.

▽ From the 1930s, the Nazis ran concentration camps to intern their opponents and other "undesirables". These included communists, socialists, trade unionists, homosexuals, gypsies and disabled people, as well as Jews. Many died in the appalling conditions and at the hands of the brutal guards.

The Second World War

Germany's armies swept into Poland on 1 September 1939, starting the Second World War and within six weeks Polish opposition had been overcome. In 1940 Hitler's campaign against France, Belgium, the Netherlands, Norway and Denmark also met with a speedy victory. Britain was left alone in the fight against the Nazis. Hitler extended his Third Reich to Northern Africa and Eastern Europe, which brought him into conflict with his former ally, Stalin. In 1941 Hitler's armies attacked the Soviet Union, in order to gain *Lebensraum* (living space) at the expense of the "inferior" Slavs. A few months after this, the United States joined the war against Hitler.

After initial victories, Hitler's advances on the Eastern Front were halted late in 1942. After this the German armies were on the defensive and were slowly driven out of the conquered territories. Early in 1945, the combined Allied forces of the Soviet Union, the United States and Britain reached the borders of the Reich. By April 1945, hemmed in on all sides by the advancing Allied armies, Hitler committed suicide in his Berlin bunker headquarters. The Thousand-Year Reich had been defeated, but some 60 million people had died.

East and West

After the end of the Second World War Germany was divided into two separate states. East Germany became a satellite of the Soviet Union, along with the other Eastern European countries. West Germany was allied to Western Europe and the United States. It received economic help from the West and rebuilt its economy. This became known as the "economic miracle".

🟨	British zone and sector
🟫	Soviet zone and sector
🟧	French zone and sector
🟩	US zone and sector
〰	1945 German frontier

The map shows the division of Germany and Berlin into four zones. The Soviet zone became East Germany while the US, British and French zones became West Germany. Germany lost a lot of territory after the Second World War. Large parts of eastern Germany were lost to Poland, which in turn lost territory to the Soviet Union. The Soviet Union was determined to have buffers between itself and Germany.

The postwar division

Early in 1945, the Allied leaders met at Yalta, on the Black Sea in the Soviet Union, to discuss the postwar future of Europe and the world. The Allies decided that Germany should be divided into zones of occupation and run by an Allied Control Commission in Berlin. It was also decided that all Germans with Nazi Party links would be excluded from power and that Germany would pay reparations to the victorious powers.

After the surrender in May 1945, Germany was divided into military zones: the Soviets kept control of eastern Germany, the British took the northwestern parts, including the industrial area of the Ruhr, and the Americans took the south. After the Potsdam conference held outside Berlin in July-August 1945, a French zone was added and Berlin was divided into four sectors of occupation, although it was located in eastern Germany. The victorious Allies agreed that the military should rule over the Germans until the Allies were satisfied that Germany had become stable and peaceful.

△ In 1945, Germany was full of "displaced" people: in the photograph, people await evacuation from Bamberg in central Germany back to their homes in the Saarland in July 1945. As the fighting got close to their homes, many Germans fled. There were also millions of foreigners in Germany who had been forced to work in German war industries as Germany ran out of workers. In 1946, millions of Germans were expelled from their homes in Poland and Czechoslovakia. Neither of these countries wanted another war in which Germany tried to regain German-inhabited territory.

Destruction and chaos

Germany had been terribly damaged by the bombing and street fighting of the war. The country had lost some four and a half million people, but nine million Germans poured into the western zones as refugees from the east. Also, only 30 per cent of its industry had been destroyed beyond repair. Thus, Germany had the industrial potential to feed itself and even to pay for reparations. However, without raw materials it could neither produce nor export anything. The lack of raw materials led to hardships, disputes, strikes and further economic chaos.

The Soviet Union, which had been dismantling German factories and machines and sending them back to the Soviet Union, stopped this policy. They were afraid that they would damage Germany so much that it would be unable to pay more reparations. It was clear that Germany badly needed economic aid to buy raw materials, as well as currency reform to restore confidence in the German mark and to end the bartering system and the black market.

Free elections

In 1946 the Allies permitted the first free elections in the regions under their control. Stalin also allowed elections in his zone, but when they failed to produce a communist victory he no longer insisted on free elections. In Berlin the Social Democrats won the local election, and they were forced to join with the Communists to form the Socialist Unity Party (SED). The SED, along with its allies always got 99 per cent of the vote in subsequent elections.

Eastern Germany and East Berlin differed from the Western zones politically. In 1948, the United States granted massive aid to the Western zones, known as the Marshall Plan. Shortly afterwards, the United States and Britain introduced a German currency reform so that the Western zones had a new, stable Deutschmark. At the same time the Soviets walked out of the Control Commission and ended the Allied rule of Germany. They also informed the West that the motorways linking Berlin with the Western zones were being closed for repairs. The Western Allies began to airlift food and fuel to West Berlin. A crisis quickly developed as the Soviets threatened to respond with military force, but they drew back, and by 12 May 1949 the blockade of Berlin was lifted.

The Marshall Plan
In June 1947, American Secretary of State George Marshall announced a plan of economic aid to restore Europe's economy. This would help Europeans rebuild their economies so that they could provide a market for American goods as well as somewhere for Americans to invest money. The plan was also political. It was aimed at containing communism and promoting "free" economic growth. Stalin immediately boycotted it as he saw it as an American attempt to dominate Europe. The Marshall Plan did, however, help Europe's economic recovery after the war.

◁ In January 1946, free elections were held in Germany for the first time since 1932. These were local elections held in the American zone. The electors chose who should represent them in their villages and towns.

▽ Women clear the rubble from in front of the Socialist Unity Party headquarters in East Berlin in November 1946. The Socialist Unity Party won the local elections held in September and October that year. By November, local government was in German hands but it took another two years before Germans took over the running of central government. By this point the country was divided into two: democratic and communist.

The Cold War

This was the public beginning of the Cold War (the conflict between the democratic West and the communist East) which had been in full swing for at least two or three years. The division of Germany into East and West was finalised in 1949 and West Germany (called the Federal Republic of Germany) was allowed to become a fully democratic country with a capitalist economy. East Germany became a "people's democracy" with a centrally planned economy, after rigged elections in which the communists won.

In the West, economic recovery was rapid, even described as miraculous, while in the East it was slow and never really accomplished, since the Soviets did not want to invest in and aid the DDR (*Deutsche Demokratische Republik*). However, the Soviets and the Eastern European countries (which had also been occupied by the Soviet army at the end of the Second World War) had to subsidise East Germans and keep their living standards artificially high so that they did not run away to the West. Later an "iron curtain" of barbed wire and minefields was built along the border between the East and West.

Reconstruction

Politically as well as economically, West Germany recovered swiftly. The new electoral law favoured a two-party system: the newly-formed conservative party, the Christian Democrats, dominated West German politics at first, with the Social Democrats in opposition. At the end of the 1960s, the Social Democrats came to power, with the Christian Democrats in opposition. A centre party, known as the Free Democratic Party, stood between the two main parties. By allying itself with the one or the other party, it was able to share power with them. Since the war, West Germany, unlike the Weimar Republic, has been a politically stable state with a flourishing economy.

In the East, political stability was achieved by Stalin's totalitarian methods: rigged elections, a one-party state, secret police and bureaucratic domination. The army also tried to keep the population firmly within the borders. In 1953 there was unrest in East Berlin and other centres and Soviet troops had to intervene to save the communist system in East Germany. German workers demanded free elections for a united Germany and at least 267 people were shot by the security forces.

Economically the DDR was floundering: cheap Chinese and Vietnamese imports replaced German-produced goods.

East Germans still left in droves: some 2.7 million left between 1949 and 1957. So in 1961 the East Germans built a wall with watch towers in the heart of Berlin to stop people leaving.

In time the communist leaders became corrupt and self-seeking, especially when the prosperous West Germans offered them economic advantages for political concessions. A flourishing trade in hostages grew up: West Germans had to pay handsomely in Deutschmarks for their relatives' freedom. Publicly, the West German government kept its distance from its East German compatriots. However, it conducted illicit trade with East Germany and even gave it some economic aid to avoid or delay a harsher economic or political climate developing there.

▽ In November 1961, the East Germans built a wall in central Berlin. This section was built in front of the Brandenburg Gate – a monument which had been built in the late 18th century to celebrate Prussia's victories. The wall divided Berlin in two and was heavily guarded to prevent people escaping from East Germany. It also prevented relatives and friends from seeing each other.

Easing the tension

In the 1970s the West Germans decided to abandon the Cold War attitudes of not recognising East Germany and the other Eastern European communist countries. Chancellor Willy Brandt, a social democrat, launched his *Ostpolitik* (meaning relations with the East) and promised to bring about closer relations with Eastern Europe. A series of treaties followed which opened up trade relations, particularly with the Soviet Union. The Berlin question was resolved by guaranteeing West Berlin's ties with the Federal Republic, but there the friendliness ended.

East Germany wanted trade, economic concessions and some visiting rights for families, all on condition that the communist system was left intact. At the same time, the East German communist leader, Erich Honecker, decided to assist West German terrorists and continue the policy of spying on West Germany's political and economic secrets. The East German security police, known as the Stasi, proved very effective at this and supplied the Soviet secret police (the KGB) with much useful information.

△ Willy Brandt was the German Social Democratic chancellor in the 1970s. He realised that West Germany had to find a way of co-existing with East Germany. Before 1970, West Germany had publicly refused to have anything to do with East Germany. First Brandt negotiated treaties with the Soviet Union, Poland and Czechoslovakia. Then in 1972 he opened up dialogue with East Germany.

In the 1970s, some West German youths, angry with the capitalist system, formed the Red Army Faction, a terrorist organisation. The DDR gave them a base and provided them with training facilities. Some leading West German industrialists were murdered and their assassins then found refuge in East Germany.

Paradoxically, Brandt fell from power as a result of a spy scandal: his personal assistant was arrested after being exposed as a Stasi agent. By the 1980s it looked as if Germany would remain divided forever. As long as the DDR had the support of the Soviet leaders and their 360,000-strong occupation army, it remained in power.

Reunification

The appointment of a new Soviet leader in 1985 was a sign that change was in the air. After four years, the East German people started to demonstrate against their communist rulers, who soon resigned. A few months later free elections were held and the path was open for reunification.

The first glimmerings that the division of Germany was not permanent came with events in the Soviet Union. In 1985, the Soviet Communist Party unexpectedly elected a relatively young man, Mikhail Gorbachev, as its new leader. The Soviet Union was beset by massive economic and social problems and Gorbachev soon announced that he wanted to change communism. He launched a reform programme designed to modernise the Soviet Union through *perestroika* (restructuring) and *glasnost* (openness).

For the next few years Gorbachev was fully absorbed in Soviet problems: it was not enough to want to change communism from above. Despite foreign policy successes, such as the signing of arms control treaties with the United States, the Soviet economy proved very difficult to modernise. The Soviet Union began to ask for help from the West. West Germany, by now Europe's leading industrial nation, became the Soviet Union's main trading partner in Western Europe. It became clear over the next few years that the Soviet Union would not be able to prop up the East German regime for much longer. The peoples of Eastern Europe also began to realise the significance of the changes going on in the Soviet Union.

Throughout the early months of 1989, there were signs of change in Eastern Europe. In Poland, the communist government started negotiating with the leading opposition group, known as Solidarity. In June 1989 some free elections were held in Poland, and for the first time the Communist Party lost to Solidarity.

Although East Germans knew about these events from West German television, it was Hungary which set off the collapse of the East German regime. In May 1989, the Hungarians began to dismantle the barbed wires of the iron curtain that divided it from Austria. This gesture, which exposed the cracks opening up in the Eastern bloc, had other unexpected and unforeseen consequences.

The mass exodus

As soon as the iron curtain came down, East Germans began to escape across it. Throughout the summer of 1989, East German tourists in Hungary took advantage of their summer holidays and continued their journey to West Germany. There they could claim political asylum, and by West German law automatically became West German citizens. On arrival the refugees received a passport, US$125, low-interest loans, unemployment benefits, free meals and temporary lodgings. For years the East German government had allowed only its outspoken critics to leave the country. In 1987, 14,000 had left and in 1988, some 40,000 emigrated. In 1989, the scale of numbers departing made the communist government panic.

At the height of the summer, 15,000 East Germans a day crossed the border. Most of the East Germans were young, skilled workers desperate to start a new life in the more affluent West. Camps were set up in Hungary to accommodate East Germans wishing to go to West Germany. The East German leader, Erich Honecker, did nothing: he was in hospital having a gallbladder operation. Meanwhile, the West German government started putting pressure on Hungary to allow the East Germans to leave. In September 1989, the Hungarian government decided to open the border with Austria officially and by the end of October the numbers of East Germans fleeing to the West had swelled to 50,000. East German tourists in Czechoslovakia began to rush into the West German embassy in Prague, where they camped in great numbers. The Czechoslovak government decided to evacuate them by special trains to the Federal Republic, instead of arresting them on the spot, as the East Germans wanted.

△ East German Trabant cars queue up to leave their country in November 1989. The exodus of people leaving East Germany reached massive proportions by the autumn of 1989.

◁ An East German refugee hugs a West German relative after arriving at Hof Station in Bavaria, southern Germany, in October 1989. She had arrived by train from Prague, where she had camped in the grounds of the West German embassy.

The party disintegrates

Since the late summer, there had been prayer meetings every Monday outside St Nicholas' church in Leipzig. By early October the numbers attending these meetings had risen to 15,000 or even 20,000. These were the largest demonstrations held in East Germany since the 1953 riots.

In October Gorbachev visited Honecker for East Germany's 40th anniversary. Gorbachev told Honecker that if there were widespread riots, he could not rely on the help of Soviet military forces. By now the East German leaders knew reform was inevitable but were also divided as to what measures should be adopted to tackle the problems. When Honecker decided to send in security forces to use violence against the growing crowds, local officials refused to obey and stopped the order.

There followed resignations and expulsions from the party and state leadership. For a month Egon Krenz, the former security chief, was the Communist Party leader, but the party and the state continued to break down under the pressure of the people.

Journalists soon revealed to the East German public that while the leadership had spoken about socialist equality, they had lived in the lap of luxury and even had secret Swiss bank accounts. Faced with a continuing flow of people to the west, Krenz announced on 9 November the lifting of all restrictions on travel and also gave instructions to start pulling down the Berlin Wall. Many citizens of Berlin brought out hammers to help bring down the wall. There were extraordinary scenes as East Germans visited West Berlin for the first time in 28 years. The West German government gave them 100 Deutschmarks "welcome money" so they could buy presents.

△ Egon Krenz enjoyed a brief month of fame as the leader of the East German Socialist Unity Party in late 1989. He was a former security chief who became leader when Honecker fell from power. Krenz tried to contain events but was overtaken by them when journalists revealed that Honecker and his wife had lived a life of luxury. Mrs Honecker was said to have flown to Paris regularly to have her hair cut. The communist leaders were totally discredited.

◁ The Soviet leader, Mikhail Gorbachev (left), greets East Germany's Erich Honecker during the 40th anniversary celebrations of the founding of the German Democratic Republic. During the visit Gorbachev made it clear to Honecker that East Germany could not rely on Soviet troops to deal with any unrest. Shortly after the visit Honecker was ousted from the East German leadership and replaced.

It was clear that the communists were losing their grip on the state. In December 1989 an extraordinary meeting of the Socialist Unity Party elected Gregor Gysi as its new leader, changed the name of the party and expelled all the compromised leaders. It also endorsed a previous decision to hold a free election in East Germany to allow the people to decide on which party should govern the country. In addition, the party agreed to reform the economy and proposed some kind of confederation with West Germany as the way forward.

Free elections

Within a matter of weeks, the communist system had collapsed. The Leipzig demonstrations swelled to enormous proportions: more than 300,000 met on Monday nights to protest against the communist leadership. The communists appointed a new prime minister, Hans Modrow, who began a reform programme. The political police, the Stasi, was dissolved by the government and then its headquarters were sacked by demonstrators eager to destroy the files kept on East Germany's citizens.

▽ East Germans demonstrate against the communists in Leipzig in February 1990. Here they are shown holding placards of Willi Stoph, Honecker's second in command, in convict's clothes. These mass demonstrations took place every Monday during the winter of 1989-90.

East Germans continued to leave their country in droves with 2,000 a day crossing the border to the West.

Demonstrators on the streets began to ask for the reunification of Germany. The slogan changed from *"Wir sind das Volk"* ("We are the people") to *"Wir sind ein Volk"* ("We are one people"). In the end Modrow had to call for a coalition government with the opposition so that East Germany could survive peacefully until the election, scheduled for June 1990.

This election was brought forward to March 1990 and brought about an unexpected landslide in favour of a conservative coalition led by the Christian Democrat, Lothar de Maiziere. The West German chancellor, Helmut Kohl, had offered the East Germans an economic and currency union by 1 July 1990. Kohl promised that all wages, salaries, pensions and rents would be converted at the rate of one Ostmark (the Eastern currency) for one Deutschmark (the Western currency). Its actual value on the black market had been eight to ten Ostmarks to one Deutschmark. Children under 14 would be able to exchange their savings at the one-to-one rate for up to 2,000 marks. People aged less than 60 could convert up to 4,000 marks, and those over 60, up to 6,000 marks. All other savings would be converted at a two to one rate. This offer went against the West German Bundesbank's advice, but the Federal Republic, under Kohl's leadership since 1982, could afford the $100 billion reunification was expected to cost in hard cash.

On 22 June 1990 both German parliaments approved the treaty on economic union, which took effect on 1 July as planned. The Western "social market system" was introduced in the East as well, the Deutschmark became the common currency and West German welfare laws were extended to East Germany.

The drive for reunification

While the Western allies reluctantly agreed to Kohl's drive for reunification, in the rest of Eastern Europe there was consternation. Poland demanded that both Germanies sign a treaty guaranteeing its border with East Germany on the Oder-Neisse line. The Soviet Union raised the problem of the military status of the reunified Germany. Gorbachev wanted either a neutral Germany, or the two Germanies remaining in their alliances, the North Atlantic Treaty Organisation (NATO) for West Germany and the Warsaw Pact for East Germany.

△ West Berliners met in East Berlin's Alexanderplatz in January 1990 and brought with them a giant inflatable banana. It was a symbol of the kind of everyday goods that were unavailable under the communist regime. In fact, many East Berliners bought bananas with their "welcome money".

▽ As soon as the communist regime started to collapse, Helmut Kohl, the West German chancellor, started to talk about German reunification.

▽ The first free elections in East Germany took place in March 1990. The Social Democrats had been expected to do well. In the event, they came second to the Christian Democrats. Both parties were helped enormously by their West German counterparts, which supplied money to fund the election campaigns.

In July 1990 Kohl visited the Soviet Union and his talks with President Gorbachev went well. They concluded an historic agreement which made sure reunification would happen in 1990. According to this agreement a united Germany would be free to join NATO. The 360,000 Soviet troops stationed in East Germany would be evacuated within three to four years. During this period NATO troops would be kept out of East Germany, while US, British and French garrisons in West Berlin would remain until the Soviet evacuation was complete. By then the combined German armed forces would be cut to 370,000 and a united Germany would renounce making or stationing nuclear, chemical and biological weapons. Kohl paid for these Soviet political concessions by offering up to US$3,000,000,000-worth of credits and a comprehensive economic pact to be signed in the future.

With this last stumbling block out of the way, the United States, Britain, France and the Soviet Union renounced their rights over Germany as the Second World War victors. On 3 October 1990 East Germany ceased to exist. The new united Germany officially became the Federal Republic of Germany and Kohl became the first chancellor. In December 1990 Kohl's Christian Democrats won the largest share of the votes in the first German-wide election held since 1932. Germans had overwhelmingly endorsed reunification.

Fears and hopes

After 40 years of division, the reunification of Germany cannot be achieved overnight. There are many differences between East and West and the economic problems are formidable. Reunification will be expensive for the West Germans.

△ Some West Germans were unhappy about reunification and protested against it in Berlin in October 1990. They were worried that they would pay more taxes and the East Germans would take their jobs.

Despite the popular enthusiasm which greeted the initial demands for reunification, there are now doubts in both East and West. West Germans are worried about how much reunification is going to cost and East Germans fear the loss of their social benefits. East Germans feel their country has been swallowed up by their economically powerful compatriots and that they will become second-class citizens. Until the East German economy has been rebuilt, these feelings will remain.

The East and West economies

East Germany had a communist economic system which is often called the command economy. Under the communist system the East German state controlled all the factories, mines and other businesses. The government told the factories what to produce, how much to sell their goods for and how much to pay the workers. Land was taken over by the state and organised into collective farms. Rents and prices of goods were subsidised. People had low wages but food and housing were cheap so they could save money. However there was not much for the people to buy. There was little unemployment but some jobs were there because they gave people work.

△ East German youths hold a banner proclaiming "Germany united fatherland" – the ironic words of the East German national anthem – during the reunification celebration on 3 October 1990.

West Germany has had a market economy for 40 years. It is one of the world's most successful economies. Most of its industry is in private hands and prices and wages are set by negotiation. Employers and unions representing workers negotiate on a wage rate after comparing it with rates in other companies and taking into account how much the cost of living has increased since the last rate was set. When they cannot agree on a rate, workers may decide to stop working and call a strike until their demands are met.

Prices are set after taking into account costs, such as wages for workers and materials, as well as allowing for a profit to be made. West Germany has a successful economy because it sells its goods abroad and its companies make good profits.

The problems

Merging East and West Germany economically will be very difficult. Much of East German industry is out of date and unprofitable. Many of the factories are closing down because the goods they produce are not what people want to buy. Some companies, especially chemical companies, are closing down because they are a danger to the environment. This means a lot of people will be out of work. In 1990 25,000 people a week lost their jobs and it was thought that as many as three million would be unemployed by the end of 1991.

Some East German companies already compete with Western companies and are successful. They include printing equipment manufacturers, machine and machine tool companies, gear-grinding machine companies and optical goods and instruments manufacturers. However, the steel companies will find it difficult competing with other steel industries on the world market. Electronics and textiles manufacturers are also outdated. Some of the smaller companies will survive as they will find it easier to go back to being privately run and may be able to raise money for modernisation.

Although some West German companies are trying to set up joint ventures, these projects are expensive and time-consuming. Volkswagen has signed a deal with the East German car maker that produced Trabant cars. Volkswagen will invest money in the factory and it is probably the only way the workers will keep their jobs. East Germany needs large amounts of money to modernise its industry as well as to improve the roads, railways, telephone network and other outdated systems.

The cost of reunification

In 1990 East Germany cost West Germany at least US$60 billion. Some of this came from private investment but the rest was paid for in increased taxes. The first few months of monetary union were thought to have cost West Germany US$100 billion. After having exchanged their savings for Deutschmarks, economists thought that East Germans would have some 115 billion marks to spend. After years of having access to shoddy East German goods, the shops were suddenly full of West German consumer goods as West German companies hoped to cash in on this. In fact the East Germans proved cautious and spent their money slowly. Many East Germans have bought second-hand West German cars. However, the problem in 1990 was that East German consumers stopped buying East German goods, so more jobs were lost. East German companies have to find export markets for their goods.

The agreements with the Soviet Union on economic aid will probably cost at least the US$3.8 billion in manufactured goods that Germany has promised to deliver under old contracts. The cost of modernising East Germany's industry is probably in the hundreds of billions of dollars but there will be some money from the European Community to help. Also there will be savings on spending on the armed forces which will be drastically reduced from 667,400 to 370,000 troops. Reunification will probably add to inflation but it will also help economic growth.

▷ Some economists estimate that the cost over the next ten years of reunification could be as high as US$775 billion. The diagram shows how much the German Federal Bank estimates reunification will cost.

▽ There are many open-cast mines in East Germany. A major cost of reunification will be cleaning up the environmental eyesores left behind. The East Germans have used cheap, brown coal to produce electricity. When this coal is burned, it emits fumes and sulphuric acid which pollute the air and cause acid rain. Many chemical factories in East Germany use old-fashioned and dangerous methods and will cost a lot of money to replace.

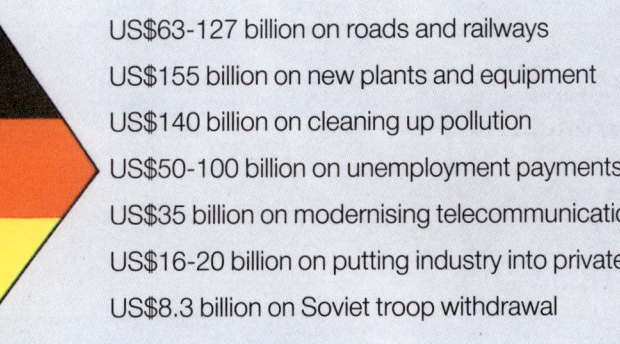

US$63-127 billion on roads and railways

US$155 billion on new plants and equipment

US$140 billion on cleaning up pollution

US$50-100 billion on unemployment payments

US$35 billion on modernising telecommunications

US$16-20 billion on putting industry into private hand⸱

US$8.3 billion on Soviet troop withdrawal

The future

The new Germany will be called upon to help its neighbours and potential enemies, Poland and the Soviet Union. There are many people in Europe who fear the emergence of a strong, united Germany. Several members of the European Community feel uncomfortable about this development. Israeli citizens are particularly disturbed by reunification, since Jewish people suffered terribly at the hands of the Germans during the Second World War. However, West Germany has had a tradition of democracy for over 40 years and is firmly part of the European institutions: the EC and NATO. The next few years will be a time of flux: foreign troops from the United States, other European countries and the Soviet Union will be leaving German territory. A new chapter in German history is about to unfold.

▽ A child looks through the remnants of the Berlin Wall at Checkpoint Charlie. This was a famous border crossing between East and West. By the end of 1990 the wall had disappeared. Reunification involves more than just knocking down the wall – much has to be rebuilt. Much East German housing is old and in need of repair. It is thought that 20 per cent of East German flats have no bath or shower and 30 per cent have no indoor toilet. It will take years for private and state money to be found to do this work.

The two Germanies

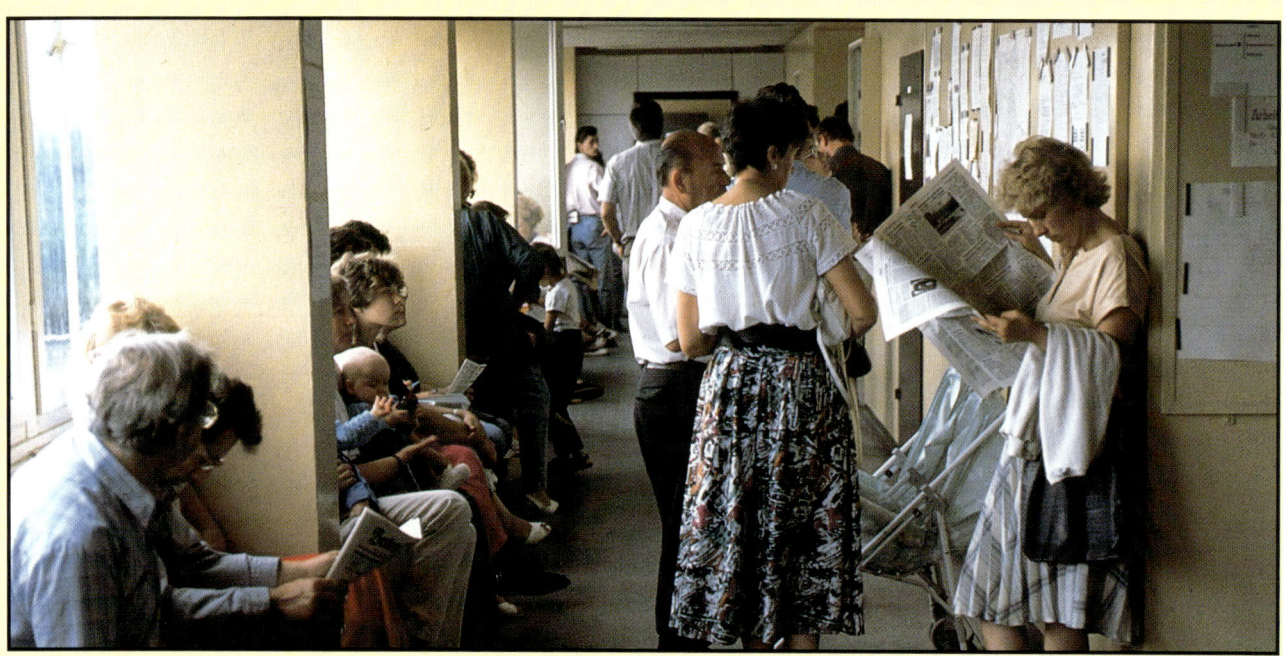

German Democratic Republic

Population: 16,340,000

Life expectancy: men: 69; women: 75

Area: 108,178 sq km: 58 per cent farming land, 27 per cent forest, 15 per cent built-up areas.

Main resources: brown coal, nickel, tin, copper, salt, natural gas, timber, potash, uranium, lead and zinc.

Main crops: wheat, rye, barley, oats, potatoes, sugar beet, carrots, apples.

Main exports: machinery, equipment and means of transport, brown coal, industrial consumer goods, food products, petro-chemical products, fertilizers, synthetic rubber, building materials.

Main imports: oil, coal and coke, natural gas, minerals, cotton, metals, fruit and vegetables, coffee, cars, raw materials for chemical products, food for livestock, sawn timber.

Foreign debt: US$13 billion

Total exports: US$31 billion

Total gross domestic product: US$207 billion

Armed forces: 173,100 troops, 335 combat aircraft, 3,140 tanks, 19 warships.

Pollution: 70 per cent of energy requirements are met by burning brown coal. Nuclear power stations also provide energy. Some 66 per cent of rivers and 23 per cent of still waters need cleaning. Heavy use of fertilizers has damaged soil. Factories release very high levels of toxic gases. Recent reports suggest that all trees are damaged by acid rain.

△ These people are waiting to talk to assistants in an employment agency in East Berlin in 1990. It is thought that at least one million East Germans were without a job at the end of 1990.

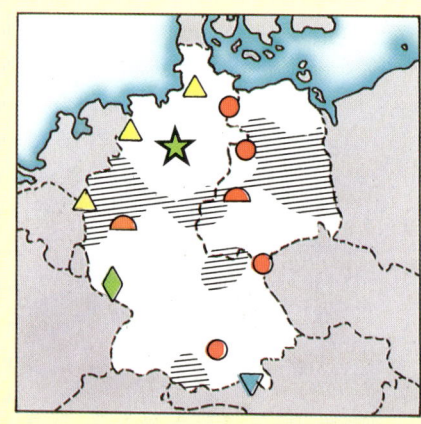

△ Lead

● Copper

▲ Nickel

◆ Uranium

▽ Bauxite

★ Silver

▨ Coalfields

Federal Republic of Germany

Population: 62,080,000

Life expectancy: men: 72; women: 78

Land area: 248,577 sq km

Main resources: coal, brown coal, petroleum, natural gas, iron ore, potash.

Main crops: wheat, rye, barley, oats, maize, potatoes, sugar beet, white beet and turnips.

Main exports: machinery, motor cars, electrical engineering and chemical products.

Main imports: foods, drink and tobacco, petroleum and natural gas, copper, bauxite, manganese, titanium, rock phosphate, wolfram and tin.

Total exports: US$323 billion

Total gross domestic product: US$870 billion

Subsidy to East Germany paid in 1989: US$12 billion

Armed forces: 494,300 troops, 507 combat aircraft, 5,005 tanks, 14 warships and 24 submarines.

Pollution: Air pollution from factory emissions and car exhausts create serious acid rain problems. Many forests are full of dying trees, for example the Black Forest. The River Rhine is one of the most polluted rivers in Europe and most of West Germany's rivers are polluted by sewage and chemicals from detergents and fertilizers. In November 1986 a fire at a Swiss factory released litres of pollution and left 100 km of the river lifeless. Each year the Rhine receives over 300,000 tonnes of waste.

West Germany already dominates the European Community economically. The united Germany will increase that domination. Although many East German companies face immense problems competing with West German industry and many are expected to go bankrupt, the West German economy is booming and reunification will increase Germany's economic power in the long run. In 1989, West Germany invested US$60 billion dollars abroad so there is plenty of money available for East Germany. However, the cost of reunification may outstrip what West Germany expected to pay.

▽ West Berlin is full of showcase architecture, such as this ultra-modern printing works. It was built to show how wealthy the West was compared to the East.

Chronology

800 AD Charlemagne crowned emperor of the Holy Roman Empire. The First Reich lasts over a thousand years.

1517 Martin Luther protests against the Catholic Church's practice of selling forgiveness; the beginning of Protestantism.

1648 The Thirty Years War, ends with the signing of the Treaty of Westphalia. Peace with France was signed at Münster.

1806 The end of the Holy Roman Empire.

1815-66 German confederation of independent states under Prussia.

1848 Revolutionary movement tries to form a unified Germany under an emperor.

1862 Otto von Bismarck becomes Prussian prime minister.

1866 Prussian-Austrian war.

1867 The Austro-Hungarian empire is proclaimed.

1871 After the defeat of the French in the Franco-Prussian War, Germany is unified: the beginning of the Second Reich.

1882 Germany, Austria-Hungary and Italy form an alliance against Russia's influence in the Balkans and Middle East.

1914 The First World War begins. Germany is allied with Austria-Hungary against Britain, France and Russia.

1918 The First World War ends with defeat for Germany and Austria-Hungary.

1919 Armed uprising in Berlin and chaos throughout Germany. The Treaty of Versailles is signed in France. Germany loses territory and must pay war reparations.

1929 The Wall Street Crash and a world economic recession.

1933 Hitler becomes the German chancellor. After the *Reichstag* fire, Hitler becomes Germany's dictator.

1938 German troops annex Austria. Hitler seizes the Sudetenland from Czechoslovakia.

1939 Germany and the Soviet Union sign a non-aggression pact. Hitler invades Poland and the Second World War begins.

1940 Germany invades and overruns Denmark, Norway, France, Belgium and the Netherlands.

1941 Germany declares war on the United States following the Japanese attack on the US naval base at Pearl Harbor.

1942 The Germans occupy much of Europe but are turned back at Stalingrad in the Soviet Union.

1945 Germany surrenders to the Allies and the war in Europe ends. The war in the Pacific ends after the atom bomb is dropped on Japan. The Soviet Union occupies much of Central and Eastern Europe.

1948-49 The Soviets blockade West Berlin: start of the Berlin airlift. West and East Germany are set up as separate states.

1953 Uprising in East Germany is crushed by Soviet tanks.

1955 West Germany becomes a member of NATO; the Warsaw Pact is formed between the Soviet Union, East Germany, Poland, Czechoslovakia, Hungary, Romania, Bulgaria and Albania.

1957 The treaties of Rome create the European Economic Community with France, West Germany, Italy, the Netherlands, Belgium and Luxembourg as members.

1961 Berlin Wall is built.

1970 West Germany and the Soviet Union sign treaties guaranteeing the existing frontiers.

1972 West and East Germany sign a treaty recognising each other's sovereignty.

1985 Mikhail Gorbachev becomes Soviet leader.

1989 Elections are held in Poland and the non-communist Solidarity wins; East Germans leave by the thousands for West Germany. The East German Communist Party loses its leading role and the Berlin Wall is opened.

1990 A Christian Democratic government is elected in East Germany. East and West Germany are reunified. Elections are held.

Glossary

Black market is the unofficial market where goods are bought and sold privately.

Capitalism is the economic system in which all enterprises are owned privately. Wealth or capital can be put to whatever use the individual wants.

Chancellor is the German equivalent of prime minister.

Coalition is a temporary alliance between different groups or political parties.

Cold War was the period of strained relations between the United States and the Soviet Union after 1945. It lasted on and off but diminished in intensity after 1985.

Communism is the belief that all private wealth should be abolished and should be held in common. In practice, the state decides who has money and fixes prices.

Democracy is a political system where people have a say in choosing or electing their government.

Dictator is someone who takes all power into his own hands and does not allow democracy.

First World War was fought from 1914-18. It was the first of the two great European wars in the 20th century. The Allies (Britain, France, Russia and later, Italy and the United States) fought the Central Powers (Germany, Austria-Hungary and the Turkish empire). The Allies won in November 1918.

Inflation describes what happens when prices for goods rise very sharply and money loses its value.

Lebensraum was Hitler's idea that Germans needed more living space in the east and should seize territory from the "inferior" Slavic peoples.

Nationalism is the belief that individual communities or cultures – usually defined by a common language – should be independent.

National Socialism or **Nazism** was the racial doctrine expounded by Hitler in Germany in the 1920s. It was a mixture of nationalism and socialism; Hitler promised to build up Germany as a nation and made promises about looking after workers' interests.

NATO is the North Atlantic Treaty Organisation, founded in 1949. It is an alliance between 16 democracies: Belgium, Canada, Denmark, Germany, France, Greece, Iceland, Italy, Luxembourg, the Netherlands, Norway, Portugal, Spain, Turkey, the United Kingdom and the United States.

Parliament is a law-making body. In a democracy it is elected by the people.

Protestantism is the religious movement of Christians who broke away from the Roman Catholic church in the 16th century.

Prussia was the leading state within Germany. Its kings were the prime movers in enlarging Prussia's territory and uniting Germany into the Second Reich.

Reich is the German word for empire. The First Reich was set up by Charlemagne and lasted until 1806. The Second Reich lasted from 1871-1918, when Germany was united under the Prussian kings. The Third Reich was proclaimed by Hitler in 1933 and lasted until 1945.

Second World War lasted from 1939-45. It was fought between the Axis powers (Germany, Italy and Japan) and the Allies (the United States, the Soviet Union, Britain, France, Australia, New Zealand and others). Germany and Japan were defeated and Europe was divided.

Socialism is the belief that wealth should be distributed more equally through taxes and that some industry should be owned by the state.

Spartacists were the extreme left-wing group who tried to seize power in Germany in 1918 and then went on to found the Communist Party.

Treaty of Versailles was the peace treaty signed at the end of the First World War by Germany and the Allies.

Warsaw Pact is a defence treaty agreeing mutual military help, signed by the Soviet Union, Poland, Czechoslovakia, East Germany, Hungary, Albania, Romania and Bulgaria.

Weimar Republic was Germany's brief attempt at democracy from the end of the First World War to 1933.

Index

Photographic Credits:
Front cover and pages 22, 26 bottom, 27 and 28-29: Topham Picture Source; pages 2-3, 30 and 31: Network Photographers; pages 4-5 bottom, 6 and 7: The Weimar Archive; pages 8, 20, 21, 22-23, 24 top and 24 bottom: Popperfoto; pages 9, 10-11, 12 top, 12 bottom, 13, 15, 17, 18: The Hulton Picture Company; pages 25 and 28-29 top: Toni Nemes; pages 26-27, 32 and 33: Frank Spooner Pictures; back cover: Roger Vlitos.